AF594608

CHEERLEADING COMPETITIONS

Candice Letkeman

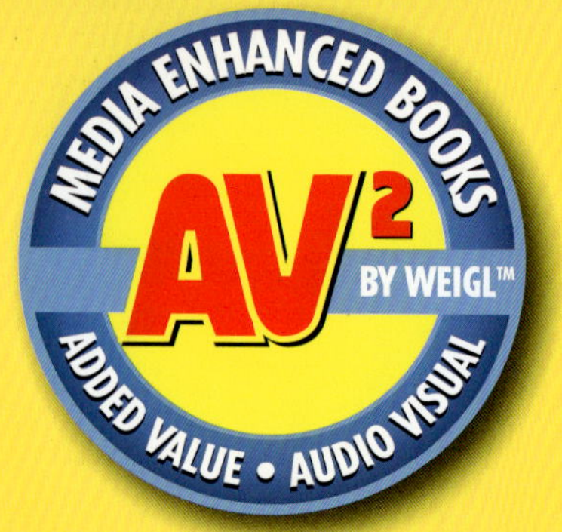

Go to www.av2books.com, and enter this book's unique code.

BOOK CODE

AVH83545

AV² by Weigl brings you media enhanced books that support active learning.

AV² provides enriched content that supplements and complements this book. Weigl's AV² books strive to create inspired learning and engage young minds in a total learning experience.

Your AV² Media Enhanced books come alive with...

Audio
Listen to sections of the book read aloud.

Key Words
Study vocabulary, and complete a matching word activity.

Video
Watch informative video clips.

Quizzes
Test your knowledge.

Embedded Weblinks
Gain additional information for research.

Slideshow
View images and captions, and prepare a presentation.

Try This!
Complete activities and hands-on experiments.

... and much, much more!

Published by Lightbox Learning Inc.
276 5th Avenue
Suite 704 #917
New York, NY 10001
Website: www.openlightbox.com

Library of Congress Cataloging-in-Publication Data

Names: Letkeman, Candice, author.
Title: Cheerleading competitions / Candice Letkeman.
Description: New York : AV2 by Weigl, [2020] | Series: Cheerleading | Includes index. | Audience: K to grade 3. |
Identifiers: LCCN 2019012101 (print) | LCCN 2019016812 (ebook) | ISBN 9781791109929 (multi user ebk.) |
ISBN 9781791109936 (Single User ebook) | ISBN 9781791109905 (hardcover : alk. paper) |
ISBN 9781791109912 (softcover : alk. paper)
Subjects: LCSH: Cheerleading--Competitions--Juvenile literature.
Classification: LCC LB3635 (ebook) | LCC LB3635 .L465 2020 (print) | DDC 791.6/4--dc23
LC record available at https://lccn.loc.gov/2019012101

Printed in Guangzhou, China
2 3 4 5 6 7 8 9 0 26 25 24 23 22

032022
110322

Project Coordinator: Heather Kissock
Designer: Ana Maria Vidal

Every reasonable effort has been made to trace ownership and to obtain permission to reprint copyright material. The publishers would be pleased to have any errors or omissions brought to their attention so that they may be corrected in subsequent printings.

Weigl acknowledges Getty Images, iStock, Shutterstock, and Alamy as its primary image suppliers for this title.

CHEERLEADING COMPETITIONS

Contents

The World of Cheerleading Competitions

Cheerleading competitions are thrilling events. **Squads** compete against each other. They perform precise moves and difficult **stunts**. Each team does its best to win. Competitions reward athletes for their talents and skills. Many competitions give them the chance to travel. They also get to see other squads in action.

Many competition costumes have themes. Costumes match the routine's music.

All types of cheerleading teams have the option to compete. **All-star** cheerleading squads exist only to compete. Some All-stars squads enter up to seven events in a year. Not all school squads are competitive.

In a competition, each team performs a routine. Each routine is set to music. Routines are judged on the difficulty of the moves. Judges also look at how well moves are done. There is a winning team in each **division**. It is usually given a trophy.

Cheerleading competitions attract dozens of teams and thousands of people who come to watch.

History of Cheer Competitions

Cheerleading competitions began in the 1960s. They were staged by the International Cheerleading Foundation (ICF). College teams battled for the awards. Each team wanted a spot on the Top 10 College Cheerleading Squads list.

All-star cheerleading started in the 1980s. All-star squads are not a part of schools. They do not cheer at sports events. Certain gyms run All-star programs. These gyms are businesses. They focus on cheerleading and dance.

The annual Pop Warner competition has been held in Florida since 1997.

The U.S. All Star Federation (USASF) started in 2003. It made rules for competitions. These include safety rules and rules on the types of moves allowed. USASF rules also explain the training coaches need. The USASF still makes rules and rule changes. Squads must be sure they keep up with changes.

POP WARNER

Pop Warner is a national program. There are classes in youth cheer, dance, and football. It is the largest program of its kind in the world. Participants are between the ages of 5 and 16. Almost half attend for cheer and dance. The program has more than 5,400 cheer and dance squads. Pop Warner holds an annual national cheerleading **championship**. More than 400 teams are featured. They compete during a five-day event at the ESPN Wide World of Sports Complex in Florida.

Cheerleading competitions were first aired on television in the 1970s.

Cheer Competitions Timeline

The first cheerleading competitions had simple moves. Cheerleaders did jumps and some **tumbling**. Today's events include complicated routines. They have thrilling stunts and dance moves.

1960s Cheerleading competitions begin. The ICF lists the top 10 college squads.

1979 Teams compete in the first high school cheerleading championship. It takes place in Memphis, Tennessee. State winners from eight states are invited.

1982 The Q94 Rockers are the first All-star team. They are from Richmond, Virginia. The team later wins the national championship in 1986.

2003 The International All Star Federation (IASF) is started. IASF makes sure all teams follow All-star rules. IASF also creates Cheerleading Worlds. This is an annual championship for All-stars.

2004 The first Cheerleading Worlds is held. It takes place in Orlando, Florida. Miami Elite wins the **coeducational** division. Cheer Athletics comes in first in the all-girl category.

2018 Cheer Athletics Claw 6 wins Cheerleading Worlds. It marks the team's 17th Worlds title. The squad is from Plano, Texas.

There are thousands of cheerleaders in Europe. Many compete at the British Cheerleading Association's annual competition in England.

How Cheerleading Competitions Work

Each competition has its own rules. Coaches and teams must know the rules for their divisions. General rules cover age limits. They give costume guidelines. There are also rules about music and time limits. Rules within each division cover jumps, tumbles, and stunts. These rules guide the quantity and quality of each move.

In many national competitions, the top 10 teams advance. They go from the semifinals to the finals. A team might perform its routine at least three times. Judges take away points from a starting score of 100. They judge routines in at least seven categories. The team with the highest score wins.

Most national cheerleading competitions last from three to five days.

Cheer Competitions Athletes and Coaches

Each competitive team has a captain. It also has **flyers** and bases. It is a base's job to hold the flyer. The base also tosses and catches the flyer. All cheerleaders are strong. They are strong physically and mentally. They must be focused and calm under pressure. They can recover quickly from mistakes.

A cheerleading competition usually has at least three judges.

Coaches are the leaders of competitive squads. Coaches create **choreography**. They teach cheerleaders how to safely do jumps and tumbling. Coaches also keep track of the schedule on competition day. They make sure the cheerleaders are warmed up and ready to perform.

The judges at competitions are cheerleading experts. They follow **criteria** for scoring. All judges' decisions are final.

Competitive cheerleaders are placed on squads by age. A junior squad might be ages 5 to 11. A senior squad might be 11 to 18.

The Right Tools

Cheerleaders go to competitions prepared to look and perform their best. They bring everything they might need on competition day.

Costumes Everyone on the team wears the same costume. Females often wear short skirts. Males usually wear long pants. Costumes are tight-fitting and stretchy. This way, cheerleaders can move easily. Many competitions require that all costumes cover the midriff when standing.

Personal Items
Hair and makeup touch-ups might be needed during a competition. A comb, hairspray, makeup, and deodorant help. They let cheerleaders look and feel fresh.

Energy-Boosting Snacks and Water Cheerleaders need to have energy and stay **hydrated** on competition day. Healthy snacks and water keep a cheerleader's energy up.

Emergency Medical Supplies Cheerleaders are prepared in the event of an injury. Athletic tape and bandages are common items kept on hand.

The Right Moves

Competitive cheerleading moves combine basic motions and jumps. Judges are looking for a variety of moves. They are also looking for challenging routines.

Toe Touch In a toe touch jump, cheerleaders keep their heads and chests up. Legs are kept straight. Then, cheerleaders pull their legs up and out to the sides. Knees face upward. Arms are outstretched like the letter T.

Layout To do a layout, cheerleaders often start by running a few steps. Then, they flip backward through the air. Their bodies stay in a straight line. They land with feet and legs together, facing the starting position.

Basket Toss In a basket toss, the bases toss a flyer into the air. Two of the bases grasp hands. This creates a cradle to catch the flyer. While in the air, the flyer can do a motion. Then, he or she falls into the cradle. A **spotter** is mandatory.

Pyramid In a **pyramid**, several stunts are done. The stunts are connected by **transitions**. Formations are made with many flyers in the air around a central flyer. The variety of pyramids is endless.

Getting Involved

Competitive cheerleaders want to win. They train and work hard. They love to perform. Competitive cheerleaders enjoy the excitement and hard work of competition. Do you have what it takes to be a competitive cheerleader?

The majority of competitions are held in the spring, but competitive cheerleaders practice year-round.

1. Watch a cheer competition to see if it interests you. Find one in your area. Many competitions sell tickets for people to come and watch. You can also watch videos of competitions online.

2. Join a competitive cheer group in your area. In All-star cheerleading, there is usually a team for everyone. Age or skill level does not matter.

3. Get fit. Eat nutritious foods. Competitive cheerleaders need to be healthy and strong.

4. Commit to team practices. You can also take additional tumbling classes and flying lessons. Extra practice can improve and increase your skills.

FITNESS PLAN

Cheerleaders have to be in strong shape for competitions. Then, they can safely do tumbling and stunts. They use a fitness plan to get strong. A fitness plan should include **cardiovascular** exercise. Running and swimming work well. Resistance training builds strength. Push-ups and squats help with this. Doing **planks** and crunches builds core strength. Core strength is needed for balance and safe landings. Daily stretching improves flexibility.

Renegade Athletics Shooting Stars

The Renegade Athletics Shooting Stars is a **special needs** team. The team is from Calhoun, Georgia. It started in 2007. The team is open to athletes ages 4 and older. All athletes are welcome, no matter their skills or abilities.

The team practices once a week year-round. Cheerleaders train according to their abilities. Coaches work with each cheerleader to build on his or her strengths.

All-star coaches are trained in CPR and first aid. Their gyms have regular safety inspections.

Renegade Athletics is an All-star gym. It is a part of USASF. The Shooting Stars began competing in 2010. Since then, the team has been in more than 15 national competitions.

The Shooting Stars have won many regional and national titles. The squad won its first national competition in 2017. The Shooting Stars have proven they can beat the best cheer teams in the country.

Like many All-star teams, Renegade cheerleaders participate in community events. These include parades, celebrations, and holiday events.

Quiz

1 Are all school squads competitive?

No

2 When did All-star cheerleading start?

In the 1980s

3 Which team won the 2018 Cheerleading Worlds competition?

Cheer Athletics Claw 6

4 How many members can competitive squads have?

Between 5 and 36

5 What is a base's job?

To hold, toss, and catch the flyer

6 What are some emergency medical supplies cheerleaders keep on hand?

Athletic tape and bandages

7 What is mandatory during a basket toss?

A spotter

8 When did the Shooting Stars win their first national competition?

2017

Key Words

All-star: a type of cheerleading in which athletes compete during routines that include advanced moves

cardiovascular: also called cardio, a type of exercise that gets the heart beating fast and hard

championship: a final competition that determines the overall winner in a sport

choreography: how performers move during a routine, usually set to music

coeducational: including both males and females

criteria: items that create a test used to judge or make a decision

division: a group of sports teams of similar age and ability

flyers: cheerleaders who are held up or tossed into the air when doing stunts

hydrated: having drunk enough water

planks: exercise moves during which push-up positions are held for periods of time

pyramid: a stunt during which cheerleaders stand on the thighs or shoulders of other cheerleaders

special needs: having physical, mental, or emotional problems and requiring extra support in education and activities

spotter: a cheerleader who watches a flyer and catches him or her if he or she falls during a stunt

squads: cheerleading teams

stunts: advanced cheerleading moves during which cheerleaders are held up or tossed in the air

transitions: the movement from one cheerleading stunt to another during a routine

tumbling: gymnastics moves, such as somersaults, rolls, and leaps

Index

Log on to www.av2books.com

AV^2 by Weigl brings you media enhanced books that support active learning. Go to www.av2books.com, and enter the special code found on page 2 of this book. You will gain access to enriched and enhanced content that supplements and complements this book. Content includes video, audio, weblinks, quizzes, a slideshow, and activities.

AV^2 Online Navigation

Audio
Listen to sections of the book read aloud.

Book Pages
AV^2 pages directly correspond to pages in the book.

Video
Watch informative video clips.

Embedded Weblinks
Gain additional information for research.

Key Words
Study vocabulary, and complete a matching word activity.

Try This!
Complete activities and hands-on experiments.

Quizzes
Test your knowledge.

Slideshow
View images and captions, and prepare a presentation.

AV^2 was built to bridge the gap between print and digital. We encourage you to tell us what you like and what you want to see in the future.

Sign up to be an AV^2 Ambassador at www.av2books.com/ambassador.

Due to the dynamic nature of the internet, some of the URLs and activities provided as part of AV^2 by Weigl may have changed or ceased to exist. AV^2 by Weigl accepts no responsibility for any such changes. All media enhanced books are regularly monitored to update addresses and sites in a timely manner. Contact AV^2 by Weigl at 1-866-649-3445 or av2books@weigl.com with any questions, comments, or feedback.